A Foreigner, Wherever I Go

by

Jon Wesick

Acknowledgements

Some of the poems in this book have appeared or will appear in the following publications: *3QR: Three Quarter Review, Cirque Journal, The Coast Highway Review, Ceremony Collected, Circle Show, Colere, De La Mancha, Diaphanous Micro, Drift wood Highway, Elohi Gadugi, Eskimo Pie, Eye on Life, Full Moon Poets Website, Land's End Bi-Coastal Poetry Anthology, Limestone Circle, Magee Park Poets Anthology, Melancholy Breakfast, Muse Apprentice Guild, New Verse News, Penduline Review, Poetry Super Highway, The Publication, Pudding, Quantum Tao, Raving Dove, San Diego Poetry Annual, Seven Circle Press, Summation, Sunken Lines, Sunken Lines Review, Synchronized Chaos, Tailvipaiva Special, Synesthesia Literary Journal, Three Treasures Zen Community Newsletter, Tidepools, Tribeca Poetry Review, Handful of Stones, Waymark, Writer's Monthly, Zillah, Time of the Poet Republic* and *Zygote in My Coffee.*

Published by Human Error Publishing
Paul Richmond
www.humanerrorpublishing.com
paul@humanerrorpublishing.com

ISBN: 978-1-948521-62-8

Illustrations and cover art by
Jon Wesick & Human Error Publishing

Table Contents

Seagulls in Their Sailors' Jackets

Dress shirts   unfolded
underwear and worn socks
on the carpet by the suitcase.
No enthusiasm for packing
or tomorrow's flight –
crowded seats, lack of sleep,
that dreary striptease at airport security.

I leave it; go to the old theater instead
where gold fixtures adorn the screen,
earrings on a silent-movie actress,
and Oscar, the duckbilled terrier,
loiters by the concession stand
bumming spare change
and scratches behind the ear.

Later unable to face the tedium
of toiletries, I choose winding stairs
and concrete sea wall. On the sand
gulls in gray pea coats huddle against
the wind. Air bladders
from shipwrecked kelp crunch
underfoot. The surf plays tag
with dry shoes. In the distance
the Encina Power Plant stands guard.
Its smokestack with flashing red light
warns airplanes away
    for now

Oceanside Idyll

Pelicans glide on the breeze
leaving no footprints in the sky.
Long beaks curl into smiles
amused by aerodynamic theories
that predict their ungainly bodies
will never fly.

Porpoises play in the waves
like old surfers reborn
with complimentary wetsuits.
Baby dolphins punctuate their joy
with leaps in the air.
The pod swims parallel to the beach
and escorts me home.

Across the Tracks

Danger
Railroad Property - Trespassing Prohibited

Nobody pays attention to the sign.
I cross the tracks feeling a little guilty.
I see more cars being repaired in dirt driveways,
        more chain link fences,
                more guard dogs with 1000 p.s.i. jaws,
                        and more brown faces
than in my neighborhood.
I don't feel threatened.
The brown faces are smiling.
Over there, grandfather is teaching *nieto*[1]
to golf in the front yard.
The boy hits the ball a few feet and shouts for joy.
An old man pushes a shopping cart
with a small rooster perched on the rim.

I'm lured into the markets
by foods with exotic names like
sopes, *chorizo*, *mole*, and *tamarindo*.
The smell of fresh tortillas greets me.
I walk up and down the aisles admiring cans with colorful
brand names: Embassa, Jumex, and El Pato.
I examine the cuts of meat most Americans won't eat:
tripa and *lengua*.

I select a few cookies and wait at the checkout counter,
while the clerk fiddles with the Lotto machine.
She asks if I know anything about computers
and invites me behind the counter to help.
We puzzle over the instructions for twenty minutes
and eventually install the print cartridge.
She gives me a complimentary ticket
and makes me promise to share the proceeds, if I win.

I don't. All I gain
is this poem. Now I must return and share it
to keep my pledge.

1. Grandson

San Diego's Old Town

Honest buildings of brick and wood stand in witness
to over a century of progress and folly. Ghosts from the past
lead children on local tours from El Campo Santo cemetery.
From under bushy eyebrows and four-star fatigue cap
General Westmoreland regards
Mrs. Bixby's third grade class.
Jimmy gets Kyle in a headlock and
bulldogs him to the ground.
Natalie runs with arms outstretched like an F-16's wings
and banks between plots outlined with picket fences.
"Ten hut!" The general bellows,
"I don't know, but I've been told..."
Children march through the wrought-iron gate
to the cadence of his voice.

A coffee-skinned boy hides behind an oak tree.
Senator Joseph McCarthy rises
from a grave marked with a simple wooden cross
and brushes dirt from his jacket's big shoulders.
"Are you now or have you ever been a member
of a terrorist nation, ethnic group, or religion?"
The young draft-dodger flees up San Diego Avenue
and stops by Diego Rivera's ladder to watch the artist
paint a monkfish on a seafood restaurant's wall.

Odysseus in khaki drives a tour bus by.
Recorded mariachi music and the aroma
of cooking tortillas waft through its open windows.
Jesus sips cappuccino in a coffee shop
across from an adobe church.
His followers fold palm fronds into roses.
All sequins, sideburns, and white leather a dozen Elvis
impersonators shake their heads at the offered flowers,
shimmy past a homeless woman and her ragged terrier,
and continue to the trolley station.
It's the best job they'll ever have. No one
will pay them to be themselves.

Bookstore by the Tea Shop

Craving cozy bookracks stocked
with Russell Banks, Milan Kundera,
and Hiroki Murakami I climb stairs, round
a corner, and find it
empty.

Lawn sculptures, potted plants,
cookbooks on tables,
and the familiar creak
of wooden floorboards
gone.

The iron laws of economics –
no more browsing before movies,
Henning Mankel,
and *Best American Short Stories*.
No more
cards with wineglass
and dark triangle of Merlot
between a woman's thighs.

The stone Buddha
once by the cash register
whispers from the past,
"Care for the present moment.
Cherish the miracles still here."

R.I.P. Del Mar Book Works 1976 – 2011

Three Dogs, a Feather, and the Homeless

Yellow, chocolate, and black Labrador retrievers,
trendy as color-coordinated sweat suits,
escort three women on their morning walk.
A sulking homeless man skulks twenty paces behind.
His grimy baseball cap floats on an ocean of matted hair.

I cross the Coast Highway to catch up.
Tongues lolling, the dogs synchronize tails to their steps.
The party stops. I pat heads and thump backs.
The dogs lean against my knees, a good omen for the day.

Later, a red light stops me in front of the retirement home.
"I don't care, motherfucker!" The bum approaches
yelling at phantoms only he sees. "Get out of my face!"
Eyes downcast like a Japanese swordsman I remove hands
from pockets to prepare for the worst and beat an SOS
on the crossing button. Slap! Slap! The bum swings
wild haymakers into his palms. My pulse accelerates.
Even imagined anger seduces.

The light changes. I ford a river of cars.
Wind suspends a feather in the crosswalk,
as if the Goddess of Mercy were dangling it
before my eyes. It floats to the pavement and tumbles
after the crazy man and the ghosts he battles.

Colorblind in Indianapolis (circa 1972)

I had it made!
Jane got on the pill,
and I was getting it
every day after high school.

She dragged me to a party,
where she guzzled underage cocktails,
flitted among the crowd,
and traded smiles with women in blue eye-shadow
and too much makeup.

The men talked about golf, real estate, and drinking.
One of the guests was running for Congress,
"to keep the niggers in line," he said.
Jane listened to the office-seeker
and nodded her head to the rhythm of slogans
like "white race" and "states' rights."

With only a glass of water for company
I sat on the couch
We left around 11:00.
I unlocked the passenger door,
while Jane staggered to my car.
"Are you going to be sick?" I asked.
"I wish you'd be more sociable," she complained.

I released the hand brake
and reached for the gear shift lever
mounted on the pale blue steering column.
When I moved the red indicator from P to R,
Jane puked.
I rolled down the window,
but all the frigid Christmas air
could not relieve the stench.

Rifle Class a Day After a Massacre

Robert Dear shoots up a Planned Parenthood clinic.
A militia takes over a wildlife refuge.
The only defense against a conservative with a gun
is a liberal with a gun
so I spend weeks in rain, hail,
and desert heat learning to shoot.

Here, on this day the screams
of the wounded are far away.
Instead hands practice the choreography
of magazine changes and malfunction clearing.
I like the rented AR-15. It's accurate,
doesn't kick much, and its loose spring
goes boing when it chambers the next round.

Hot wind sucks water from my body
and even slathered in sunscreen my face burns.
Ammo belts on women's hips distract me.
"It's too quiet," the teacher says.
"All I hear is pistols next door.
Let's show them what real firearms sound like!"
With others I center my ghost ring sight
on a gray silhouette and squeeze the trigger.
Rifles' booms alert car alarms. Dust puffs
on the berm behind paper targets.
Hot brass flies from an ejection port,
falls down my shirt, and burns.

We sling loaded rifles over shoulders only once.
"Feel something different?" the teacher asks.
"That's the feeling of freedom!"
I don't feel freedom.
I feel a rifle
and a heavy responsibility

Plains of Abraham

With macarons, duck confit, and maple syrup at stake,
I reenact General Wolfe's conquest of French Canada.
Backed by divisions of tourist dollars and a robust
exchange rate, my *anglais* marches north
toward the *français*' fortress atop a fifty-meter cliff
(but anglais doesn't know what a meter is).

A fusillade of unintelligible vocabulary
repels my attempted landing at Tim Hortons.
Grilled cheese and two-dollar coin in hand,
I flee to my *voiture*, abandoning my latte
in a panicked retreat.

My anglais gains a foothold in a hotel.
Behind makeshift defenses of cable TV
streaming CBC news and old reruns
of "Murder She Wrote," my ego prefers
the blood-soaked glove of genocide
to the shame of standing carp-mouthed
at some incomprehensible phrase.

Scouts report parapets of unpronounced consonants,
howitzers of *passé composé*, mortars of gendered nouns,
muskets of strange accent marks, and field guns
of adjectives following nouns. I know
what I must do.

In dress uniform
I march to the nearest *pâtisserie*
and stammering my first, halting
words in a foreign tongue
lay down my sword

anglais – English language
français – French language
voiture - car
passé compose – past tense
patisserie - bakery

Dancing with the Inuit

Tourists sit on folding chairs
in a high school gym north of the arctic circle.
They don't budge,
when Indians invite them to join the dance.
I also sit on a folding chair,
fidgeting because moving naturally
never came naturally to me.
I'd like to say the shaman's drum called,
but I just don't belong
with the middle-aged middle-class.
I take my first awkward steps
to the drum's rhythm
of understanding.

Wreck Beach

Take the path down the hill from UBC[1]
through gentle forests of fern and evergreen.
Follow it down to the beach and find a garden.
Women sprout nude from white sand,
grow, and ripen in the summer sunshine.
Breasts emerge from stifling bras,
forsake taunting behind obscene nylon,
and breathe the cedar-scented air.
Don't be a voyeur! Unbutton your inhibitions.
Slip out of your shorts and shyness.

I hear the sound of motors. Quick, get dressed!
A hover craft lands on the beach.
Men in the black uniforms step onto the sand.

Dozens of naked Polynesian women
walk toward Captain Cook's sailing ship
bearing gifts of flowers.

---

1.   University of British Columbia in Vancouver, Canada.

Reality

I approach the monastery of green corrugated steel in a forest of cedar and hemlock. Film badges and radiation dosimeters line the rack by the gate. I clip mine to my belt and enter. It's a typical Pacific Northwest night. The cool, misty air caresses my face with the clean smell of evergreens. I cross the courtyard and enter the meson hall. The steel door slams behind me. Inside, harsh fluorescent lights illuminate the concrete radiation shielding stacked like a giant's toy blocks by the overhead crane. Banks of power supplies fill the air with a sixty-cycle hum. My boots sound on the steel stairs as I descend to the counting room. It's midnight, and I'm here to pull a graveyard shift on experiment 208 at the TRIUMF particle accelerator.

Gordon and Harry tell me that Rudy will be late, and then they leave for their motel rooms. I read the day's entries in the logbook, record the leakage currents on the high-voltage supplies, and go downstairs to check the flow of magic gas to the wire chambers. Back in the counting room, my fingers dance over the data acquisition computer's keyboard, and a scatter plot appears on the monitor.

Here's reality at its most basic level, but it comes at the end of a chain of equipment and abstraction: A beam of protons enters an evacuated aluminum coffin and passes through a hydrogen target, affectionately known as the Hindenburg. Some of these will scatter from the target, and fewer will create a gamma ray when doing so. A fraction of the gammas leave their ghostly traces in sixteen lead-glass detectors, each the size of a cinderblock.

One outgoing proton passes through two wire chambers, an electromagnet, and another two wire chambers. Its bend through the magnet allows us to determine its momentum. Plastic scintillators inside the coffin detect the other proton. Signals pass through two racks of electronics as tall as a man, hundreds of feet of cable, another electronics rack in the counting room, and finally into the computer. By comparing the difference in the reaction rate when incoming protons are spin-up compared to spin-down, we hope to determine which of the competing nuclear forces theorists have proposed is the most accurate.[1]

A million things can go wrong. Most of them involve cables. Black coaxial cables thick as your middle finger connect all the electronics. They writhe and squirm through the cave and counting room like Medusa's dreadlocks. I've seen physicists waste eight hours of precious beam time tracking down a problem that turned out to be a bad cable. Instead of missile defense, this country should invest in a Cable Connector Initiative, not as sexy but it would pay off in saved money, effort, and frustration.

Are the fundamental building blocks of matter, which can only be observed by a team of Ph.D.s with hundreds of millions of dollars' worth of equipment, more real than my worries about how I'll earn a living after completing my postdoc next year? I look through the computer displays. A time-of-flight peak is drifting outside its windows. This could be trouble. Should I wade into the wall of electronics armed only with an oscilloscope and tiny screwdriver (to adjust trim pots), or should I wait for Rudy, who's better at fixing things. I often find myself facing this dilemma. The clock says 12:45 a.m. It's so easy to ruin the delicate timing. I decide to wait.

Staying awake until dawn takes a sledgehammer to my circadian rhythms. This jarring of my biological clock saps energy from the mental electric fence that keeps the wolf pack of inadequacy away from my ego. I feel like an imposter posing as a scientist. All those transistors in the mountains of electronics are conspiring to break down, thus revealing my helplessness, unmasking me as the fraud I am.

Someone's left a *Scientific American* behind. The cover announces this issue is dedicated to the Standard Model of particle physics. I page through an article on quarks and gluons. The theory has always sounded like something a groggy physicist would dream up at 1 a.m. A colleague told me that in the 1950s he used to work through all the articles in the *Physical Review*, even those outside his field. You can't do that anymore. Even for our modest project two theorists took six months developing a computer model to predict the results. I can follow some of the equations, but the details slip through my fingers, like sand does when scooped from the ocean bottom and brought to the surface.

My stomach growls. It's two o' clock, and my eyelids begin to droop. Whatever happened to the physics of things you can touch? It went out with the concept of electric fields in the nineteenth century. A professor of mine used to say touch is an illusion, only the electrostatic repulsion between atoms. Even so, I want to crawl into bed and feel my girlfriend's arms surround me like a warm sweater. Yet I have six hours left, six hours to stay awake and hope nothing goes wrong, six hours to pretend I'm in control of what's going on.

1. Writing an equation for the nuclear force is not as easy as writing one for gravity or the Coulomb force. For one thing, the nuclear force acts only at short distances. Also with the exception of the deuteron, nuclei contain more than two particles, so one would need to disentangle multi-particle effects to come up with a force. While the Standard Model of Particle Physics describes the nuclear force, it comes with all the complications of quantum field theory and nucleons that are composed of three quarks. Since reactions in nuclear physics take place at non-relativistic energies, physicists wanted a simpler approximation to use at lower energies. Examples are the Paris Potential and the Bonn Potential. Note that force is the derivative of potential energy

In quantum mechanics, many particles carry intrinsic angular momentum much like a spinning baseball. This is pretty weird because some of the particles, like the electron, have no size. What is there to spin? The answer falls out of the math when you combine quantum mechanics and special relativity. Anyway, for particles like protons, spins can point in one of two directions, either up or down (more correctly, you can only measure one vector component of the total spin). In our experiment, we bombarded our target with polarized protons (those having their spins aligned instead of in random directions). The normalized difference in the cross section (roughly the reaction rate) is called an analyzing power. We hoped that this would be sensitive to the nuclear potential used in the model, and that this would help choose the best nuclear potential to use when modeling nuclear reactions and nuclear structure.

Lift Off

Under the wing
       of the Space Shuttle Enterprise
              (at the Smithsonian Museum)
      a Gemini space capsule
          not much more than a garbage can
               with two seats

A child's voice
            "Wow!"
               It's a girl!
      long hair   knit cap
        face unetched by experience

    "Sorry"   she hunches her shoulders
           when I turn

    "Don't be sorry"

And I would wrap her wonder
        in an ablative heat shield
          to survive the fires of womanhood
      high heels
        her mother's lipstick
     boy's hands inside her bra

  I'd add an air supply
        to protect from suffocating cynicism
     and the poison breath of fraud

So she can build her own rocket

     Lift off
        solar systems   galaxies   nebulae
  the heavens
      hers to explore
      "Wow!"

Naropa Girls

Boulder, Colorado — Naropa Institute Summer Writing
Program.

Straightforward, no games, introduce themselves girls.
Dreadlock, dog owner, sleepin' in the park girls.
Sari wearin', forehead dot, workin' in café girls.
Green shoes, been to Europe, children's writer prose girls.
Army pants, round hips, I can see your navel girls.
Baseball hat, cute name, ass grabbed, MC girls.
Wearin' red, brought her back, celebrated author girls.
Oak tree, recent grad, $50 k in debt girls.
Dharma talk, question asking, concerned bodhisattva girls.
Rainin' hard, gave a ride, really saved my ass girls.
Natural, genuine, hope you never lose that girls.
Wish California girls could all be Naropa girls.

The Geography of Memory

Opportunity's legs stretch for miles and miles.
Its marathon of school and work whipsaws
me across North America
shattering friendships and community.
On a sprint east
I detour to my boyhood home
that L-shaped house on Columbine Lane

and recall how I built model airplanes
B-17, Spitfire, and Me-109
on a paint-splattered table
in the chilly, gray basement,
the air smelling of glue and enamel thinner.
Subsisting on Reese's Peanut Butter Cups,
sci-fi, cheese curls, and bad movies
I set world records for lack of sleep.

Nights I'd slide open
the bedroom window facing the driveway,
step onto juniper branches
heavy with waxy, blue berries
and rendezvous with DeNardo
to play bazooka
with bottle rockets and conduit pipe
as if suburban homes were King Tigers
overrunning the 101st Airborne.
Later, in boots and purple jacket
I stood nighttime vigil outside Brenda's window
while fantasizing some psychic embrace
that would open the gates of manhood.

Across Maple Avenue and through a maze of side streets
squats the old high school that tortured me
with sixth-period gym so the winter wind
froze my hair into ice cycles, hats being uncool.
Starbuck's replaced Gary's Drug Store.
The barber who cut my hair so short,
I covered my shame with a gallon of gel,
is gone but the old railroad bridge still thunders terror
from the bang and roar of overhead freights.

I've walked these streets in memory for decades
searching for loves and adventures
aborted by home leaving.
In real life, I spend an hour.
The magic that was those years - Vic's fake Russian accent,
hanging out with Gene and Chaz at the bowling alley,
and my girlfriend's job at the chicken place
now decayed
to shopping malls
and franchise blandness

My Mother's Ashes

She wanted them scattered
in the Colorado mountains
so with burning eyes I drive her remains
through blinding desert, Vegas, Utah
to the place of my birth.

Long dormant memories leach from my bones –
pure air scented with pine and sun-baked dust,
miles of tunnel cut through mountain,
the Front Range embracing the horizon,
green Sinclair gasoline brontosaurus,
mica glittering in rocks, my old aquamarine sleeping bag,
needle-like trout bones caught in my throat,
and smell of breakfast cooking on our brick grill.

No ceremony needed. She was an atheist.
But she deserves more than the slapstick
of my father's scattering. Searching, searching
for the right place. The brown Colorado River rushes
between sheer, metamorphic rock walls.
Nowhere to stop. Only the boring, flats have parking.
Finally a turnout away from gawkers
not perfect but good enough.
A butter knife pries open the black box.
I remove two pounds of fine, gray ash
in a plastic bag sealed with tie wrap and metal clamp.
Knife cuts bag. Ash dumps more than scatters.

The Bodhisattva of Vegetarianism grants me an indulgence.
I stop for barbecued ribs like those I loved as a child.
Fingers greasy despite four paper towels,
tongue probing meat caught between teeth,
I now see my parents' early optimism, how they believed
mountain-inspired decency would prevail.
What happened? What happened?

San Onofre

Trendy women suck poison from cigarettes and speed
their sport utility vehicles past warning signs depicting
                                a running family.

The Mexican family flees across traffic to evade
                    the immigration checkpoint and remain
in America with its jobs and better pay.

The INS agent at the checkpoint looks for brown faces
in car windows, while hoping to get off work soon
and practice karate with his friend.

His friend, a guard at the nearby nuclear plant, misses
his old job as a bouncer in a topless bar.

He no longer notices the two containment domes shaped
like enormous breasts, that suckle the unwanted
thirty-five-year old infant
once named
Progress.

Union Station

I can no longer be angry
when trains blast air horns
and rattle along the tracks outside my window.
Now they carry me north to LA,
that sprawling whore of a city,
who'll love you for a few bucks
and sometimes for free.

My lover waits outside the station
in her small white car with her sweet-natured dog.
We drive past broken sidewalks and Korean signs.
At home she kisses me open-mouthed.
I move closer wanting her to swallow me,
so I can live warm and protected
inside this woman's smooth flat belly.

Can't get close enough.
I return to myself and wait in Union Station
for the train back to my world and work.
I choose a leather seat far from the stale piss smell
of the bums with their stringy beards and long matted hair.
A line of gray-suited businessmen files by.
Somehow, a pigeon has fallen in with them.
He moseys along bobbing his head in time with his steps
thinking, "Just act naturally and no one will notice."

The announcer calls my train.
I shoulder my backpack
and head toward the platform,
trying to act naturally
walking, not flying.

Refuge Denied

Two girls chalk a mandala
of green leaves and pink flowers
on the asphalt by a BART station.
A skinny kid with a Mohawk
carries his guitar into the sacred circle
and screams a Clash song.
A woman with a book of poems follows
but a homeless drunk pushes her aside
with a twenty-minute rendition of
"Suck my black dick!"

Welcome to San Francisco – sacred mandala
of art and culture refuge of stylish lesbians
and Prius taxis where a North Beach dog accompanies
a park-bench sax player with barks and growls
and the godfather of Chinese Tea
cajoles his patron over tiny cups
of Pu-Erh and High Mountain Oolong.

At the Zen Center a *cholo jisha*
with soul patch and baggy jeans
carries incense for a black-robed priest.
Panhandlers give high fives and broken-toothed smiles
to passersby who travel sidewalks that glitter
like the Milky Way.

San Francisco, whose lifeblood is money.
Smell it on the gray-haired man
who wears a twenty-year-old blond like a Rolex,
the kind of woman who'd turn her back
if I said hello.
Still, traces of old San Francisco remain.
Plodding up Powell Street Laura Linney
smiles at me while gasping for breath.

San Francisco, beautiful dream on the verge
of self-destruction where prices are obscene
where restaurant bills shout, "Suck my black dick!"
and rents sell your mother into prostitution.
San Francisco, an escape from corporate America
affordable only by the masters of corporate America.
San Francisco, I love you but
only the rich can find refuge here.

Death Valley Traffic Jam

Cars and trucks choke the freeway,
spoiling my four-wheel dream
of an open road in the most desolate place on earth.
My friends and I inch along
a concrete ribbon in my new compact.
Southwest of Las Vegas
I play tag with an aircraft-carrier-sized motor home.
A cardboard Wile E. Coyote grimaces
from the Eisenhower's grill
like the drivers in today's log jam.

I steer down an exit.
Vrrmp! Wheels vibrate over a cattle guard.
Soon we're surrounded by space
sagebrush, creosote, Joshua trees,
and spiny yucca our only neighbors.
We breathe stillness.
The setting sun plays blue on distant peaks
through a gap in rare gray clouds.
The line of cars we left
crawls from horizon to horizon
like ants swarming my coffee cup.

We rejoin the exodus only to move in lock step
with gamblers, returning from casinos
that resemble new car showrooms
in their glitz and distraction.
I strain to see around another 15 gallon-per-mile SUV.
Wagering on a vision of progress,
America rolls snake eyes again and again.
Lured by phantom freedom from a TV ad,
He raises the stakes with each loss.
When you toss dice in Motor City,
the house always wins.

A Treasury of Banter

My neighbor knocks. "Got a pen?"
"You don't have a pen?"
"100% digital, my friend, 100% digital."
That's how it goes in Massachusetts,
land of Dunkin' Donuts, Celtic music on the radio,
and cheese pizza more heavenly
than anything on Brillat-Savarin's table.

An Asian woman, whose staid blouse
and glasses whisper "classical musician,"
stomps like a raging Maori
while the amplifier blasts Harvard Square
with punk-rock chords from her violin.
A black teen rockets his skateboard
over the curb and confides,
"Never thought I'd make it."

An Arab grandmother sits in Boston Common,
cuts plums into wedges,
and passes them to son and his children.
Trees, promenade, and swan-shaped boats
transform into Seurat's "Sunday Afternoon."

By Thoreau's cabin, ducks, fishing lines,
and swimmers fill Walden Pond.
Attempting to add a capstone,
I capsize pagodas of rocks
erected by admirers more skillful than me.

"How you doing?" I hand the clerk my Cabernet.
"I'm like Mohammed Ali," he says,
"They beat the shit out of me
but I keep fighting."

Wandering Manhattan

A Sumerian sage exits the Metropolitan Museum and buys falafel from one of the halal food carts lining Fifth Avenue. Yogurt sauce dribbles down the ringlets of his chest-length beard and onto his lapis lazuli necklace as he walks and eats. Three Abrahamic religions follow. Each time a clay tablet falls from his satchel, they grind the cuneiform to dust under their heels.

"Hey, see that Sumerian sage eating falafel?" I ask a woman in silver, platform boots. She does not look up from her smart phone.

Leaving the religions behind, the sage plunges into the swirl of garbage trucks and kamikaze bicyclists with no regard for crossing lights. Keeping his fish-shaped hat in sight, I place my trust in Enki, step into the intersection, and emerge unscathed. I follow him to Hell's Kitchen and past the appetizers it offers: Uzbek dumplings, Korean fried chicken, stuffed grape leaves in walnuts and yogurt, cold-brewed nitro coffee, hand-pulled noodles, and cardamom tea served by an Afghani who greets customers with, "Hello, my friend!"

I catch up to the sage by a poke-bowl restaurant as he mutters something in a language with no modern analog. Perhaps he's having second thoughts about the invention of the city at Uruk or maybe he's complaining about the lack of public bathrooms, which reminds me...

I duck into a Starbucks but find only a counter with no chairs let alone toilets. Responsible businesses would recycle the fluids they sell. There ought to be a law.

Back on sidewalk, a balding smoker, who limps more slowly than continental drift on crutches, blocks my path. Bloated gut, sagging pants, and swollen ankles – I see my future. Even though my bladder spasms an SOS in Morse code, I don't body-check him into the black, garbage bags on the curb.

Hole in the Sky

Swells of cumulus part
because this is no hour
for "ordinary miracles."
As the moon nibbles our star,
the orange sunset overhead pours
otherworldly light on street,
lawn, and deck chairs.

The moon covers more, more
     until
"God's miracle!"   Totality

Crickets sing.   An onyx
set in burst of white gold hangs
in the sky
like an alien spacecraft
with propulsion beyond
human understanding.

Protective glasses cover eyes again.
Goddess Sun also known as
Amaterasu Ōmikami, Wuriupranili,
Shapash, Atanua, Chup Kamui,
or simply photons squeezed by gravity
from a ball of hydrogen
reemerges wearing her rarest jewel
a fingernail sliver
of ruby

Full Eclipse, Columbia, South Carolina, August 21, 2017

The Key

fits the lock of the old-fashioned door
        that rattles when closed.
The door separates our love making
        from the hallway of the bed and breakfast.
You spotted the B&B from my car
        amid mouthfuls of blueberries.
We bought the berries
        at a roadside stand in Nova Scotia.
The road parallels the shore of the dark blue Atlantic
        and eats my cash faster than planned.
My cash flow prompts you
        to offer your credit card,
but your card has exceeded its limit.
        You say that's what happens with poor girls,
poor girls who need to pay for college,
        so they enlist in the army.
The army will dye your life olive drab
        and send you away to Germany.
Germany will change you, and
        even though I visit, things will never be the same.

Somewhere in the Yucatan

The driver of the second-class bus accepts my ticket,
even though it's for first class.
I choose not to wait another half hour for tinted windows.
Surrounded by blinking Christmas lights,
                    a portrait of the Virgin Mary
watches over us from above the driver's head.
We cruise a bit then pull over at a red, white,
                    and green cement bus stop.
An old woman boards and takes the seat beside me.
She has dark skin and a nose like a parrot's beak;
wears a *huipil*[1] with a human skull pattern;
and balances a basket of corn, chilies,
and chocolate on her lap. Scars
left by her Spanish ex-husband decorate her face.

The driver's in no hurry. He swaps jokes with his friend
and makes time with the slender brunette in the front seat.
Our bus bounces down the road past palm trees and shacks
to the rhythm of Mariachi music from the driver's boom box.
America sits behind me and whispers,
"How will you get from the bus station to your hotel?"
My mind rehearses Spanish phrases for the cab ride.

I turn when a calloused hand taps my wrist.
The old woman points out the window
at a burro plodding along the road.
She reaches into her basket, withdraws two candies,
and hands one to America and another to me.

I abandon thoughts of the future.
Distracted by the bittersweet Mayan chocolate,
America remains silent for now.

1. A multicolored Mayan blouse.

Tourist Season Runs from March through February

All hotels   booked

I rent a phone booth instead

Central Amsterdam   200 euros a night   Sweet!

except

whenever I change clothes

someone yells, "Lex Luthor is robbing

the Raadhuisstraat Savings and Loan!

Come quick!"

Woman Under Glass

Red lights
fluorescent and horizontal
above black-framed picture windows
where women pose in bikini underwear.
Blonde   statuesque with honey-colored skin
here and there a sympathetic face
flat bellies   curved hip
breasts in low-cut bras.
Some women break the fourth wall
leaning out of doorways to smoke and chat.

A young man pumps his fists with enthusiasm
and goes inside to negotiate a price
while unconcerned police in white shirts
loiter by the old church. Guides carry flags
to lead Japanese tourists through narrow alleys.

The Dutch seem unfazed.
Neighbors of sex workers picnic
on steps overlooking canals.
Porn shops, live sex shows
not as important as conversation
and glasses of dry white wine.

Slices of aged Gouda and fresh bread.
Taste the rich smoked salmon.
Tell me about your day

Still Life with Tourist's Head

The scene depicts a bounty of fruit obscured
by a large head in the foreground.
A pear resembling a woman's breast
just behind the right ear draws the eye
as if the artist were saying
all that separates the viewer
from a natural state of bliss
is that damn head in the way.

Instead of the short brush strokes
in contrasting colors of the background
the artist painted the head in photographic detail.
The dandruff-laden hair circling the bald spot
brings to mind a swastika and a precancerous mole
sprouts like skunk cabbage from the tourist's neck.
One can almost hear the heavy metal guitars
blasting from his ear buds.

Art historians have proposed several interpretations.
Perhaps it reflects the artist's commitment
to painting life as it is. Perhaps
it was a comment on postmodernism.
Whatever the artist meant
heads blocking views
became the rage in the art world.
Just visit any museum

Dutch Postcards

Hair stuffed under a Rasta cap
Anne Frank smokes a bong
and nods to the reggae beat.
Eyes staring   unfocused
her gaze lingers too long on me.

She's there at Coffeeshop Resin,
Barney's, the Free World, the Bulldog,
Double Reggae, Popeye's, Kadinsky,
the Doors, Abraxis, Grey Area, Easy Times,
Relax, Picasso, and the Other Side
examining buds under a magnifying glass
and talking price with a man in black hat,
Van Dyke, and ruff collar.

She hands out samples of Gouda
at cheese shops, nearly runs me over
when I'm not watching for bicycles,
and sings Leonard Cohen's "Hallielujah" in the square.

Posing half naked behind a window
in the red light district she taps the glass
to get my attention and rubs her belly
when I turn.

She follows me on the train to The Hague
and points to postcards in a shop outside the station.
I buy a dozen and address them to John Yoo,
Dick Cheney, and other torture apologists.
"At the International Criminal Court.
Wish you were here!"

Brugge Hospitaalmuseum

In a medieval town
a medieval hospital
only a warehouse for the dying
back then

Now a museum
with tipped, arched windows
and paintings by Hans Memling
minute detail and awkward perspective
in oil on wood

Upstairs
the roof an overturned boat
with dark oak ribs.
101 black-and-white portraits
faces from birth to age 100 on display
Your face   my face

I examine
how children turn into persons
freckles   dimples,
the 16-year-old girl
I would have liked to know
when I was her age

Where is the border
between growing
and dying?

Crow's feet, sagging flesh,
the vacant look in hound-dog eyes

I Attend a Poetry Reading in Western Ireland

The empty seats up front   occupied
by ghosts from the potato famine.
Next rows martyrs
from the Easter Uprising,
War of Independence, Civil War,
and Northern Ireland Troubles.

No place for me
to sit
so next to Maud Gonne[1]
I stand in back
dropping and retrieving
umbrella, jacket
books

1 W.B. Yeats' unrequited love.

Smiles Under the English Channel

Sleek train slips
into the channel tunnel
100 miles per hour.
The woman carries a toddler to their seat.
Tiny arms reach through long brown hair
encircle her neck, his head nestling a shoulder,
left bare by her red halter. Soon he abandons mom
to bounce down the aisle. Short legs give out.
He lands on his bottom. Eyes wide with shock
he stares up at me. Pink pimples on his cheeks
Chicken pox???
I say, "Boom!
Boom!"
He opens his mouth in a grin,
places a warm tiny hand on my leg,
hoists himself up, and resumes
zigzag wobbling up the aisle.

Eyes shining behind oval glasses,
mother sings "Gaspar!" to call him back.
Nanoseconds later he's on another expedition
this time investigating Japanese tourists.
A tiny woman asks him, "*Dochira ikimasu ka?*"
An African with a shaved head says, "*Tiens!*"
and summons the boy with a tinny tune on his cell phone.
He places Gaspar on the knee of his creased slacks
and recites stories in French.

Instead of the usual spasm of shoving luggage
passengers linger on arrival.
I wish the French backpacker, "*Bonne journée.*"
A Japanese bows to the African.
From his seat on mother's lap
Gaspar smiles.

A Paris Hotel

A phalanx of ebony-skinned prostitutes
eager to make the gutters run with semen
lies in ambush along Rue d'Aboukir.
One aims spandex-covered breasts at me,
bats blue-caked eyelashes,
and whispers, "*Ça va?*" through greasy painted lips.
When I walk past, she hollers, "*Attendez!*"

The concierge fingers the stubble on his chin
and speaks with a gravelly voice.
"You American? Okay, pay me cash tomorrow."
I trudge the frayed carpet up seven flights
of narrow stairs to my penthouse.
Three hundred francs[1] buys a collapsed mattress,
peeling paint, toilet, shower,
and a sign forbidding clothes-washing.

A dusk breeze carries distant French
and Arabic conversations through my window.
I step onto the balcony. Chimneystacks sprout
a strange forest from Paris' mansard roofs.
I gaze through apartment windows
imagining the tenants' lives.

The city's buildings expand and contract,
drawing breath through doorways and Gothic arches.
The living organism covers the entire continent.
Europe looks at me with tired eyes

1. About $40 at the time

Remembering Oscar

A woman bends toward the monolith
and places a kiss
of acceptance on the rough white stone.

Rest now.
Your persecution is over.
The rusty iron bars that eclipsed your light
in the damp Victorian prison cell
are only a memory.

Gardeners tend flowers in the Paris sun.
Red and pink outlines
       of a hundred lips
            adorn the tomb.

Suomenlinaa

The artillery faced east
when Sweden owned it.
The Russians took over
and turned the guns the other way.
They left eighty years ago.

It drizzled earlier, but
a heavy storm never materialized.
It's a great day
to eat a slice of fairy tale cake at an outdoor café
while viewing Helsinki's black roofs
and onion domed churches across the harbor.

Even better
spread a blanket among the yellow flowers
that grow everywhere
obscuring the old fortress walls.
Rest your head on your lover's lap.
Feel her through the thin summer dress.
Smell the lavender blossoms.
Watch the clouds move across the sky
or look at the child sitting atop
an obsolete cannon.

Suomenlinna is an island in Helsinki's harbor. The Swedish
fortified the island in 1748 to defend against Russia. Russia
conquered the island in 1808.

Parting Gifts

Estonia lost a large part of its population after being invaded by both the Nazis and Soviets during WWII. During the Soviet occupation from 1944 to 1991 the authorities attempted to dilute Estonia's culture by moving lots of Russians there. After independence in 1991 30% of Estonia's population consisted of unwanted ethnic Russians.

Cement block apartments litter the highway
from my hotel to Tallinn's old town.
Leftovers from Estonia's former Soviet occupiers
drab peeling paint and weathered wood.
Rusty padlocks
secure sooty abandoned factories behind chain-link fences.

Someone's installed a nightclub in one.
The green sign and blue awning emerge from a mass
of broken windows, rubble, and blackened smokestacks.
Free enterprise brings gas stations and traffic jams.
Trendy shops compete for tourist dollars
along the medieval city's convoluted cobblestone streets.

A sign requests donations for renovations
inside the big Russian Orthodox church
across from the pink parliament building.
Why give money to those who enslaved my ancestors?
Still, I admire the huge chandeliers, vibrant icons,
and sky-blue ceiling with six pointed gold stars.
I drop a coin in the box.

Later, a sudden thunderstorm pelts me with rain.
I take cover in an art gallery.
A handsome young man in a straw hat
has been stranded too.
He asks about my taste in music,
says he plays drums in a rockabilly band,
and tells me he's one of the Russians
left behind after the Soviet pull-out.

The storm clears.
I tire of trying to comprehend his halting English.
He struggles on
attempting to communicate long after I would have quit.
He stammers, "Now Eesti parliament - Russians..."
and kicks his foot like booting a piece of garbage
from his path.

Rasputin joins us. He tears the cap
from a vodka bottle and throws it away.
"Let's go this way." He points down a deserted alley.
Fearful for my ticket home
in the money belt chafing my belly
I make excuses, walk away, and duck into a café
to make sure they don't follow.
I realize ethnic cleansing's cause
sometime between the main course and dessert.

The Gift of the Trees

Palanga, Lithuania

Blond men with crewcuts swig beer from brown bottles
and escort long-legged women in short skirts
along tree-lined flagstone sidewalks.
At first you think the women wear red stockings,
but it's only sunburn from the 18-hour days.
Amplified music blares from a dozen cafes
and combines into an incomprehensible cacophony.
The clop-clop of horses' hooves
announces the return of a cart with its cargo of sightseers.
Merchants' tables display amber necklaces, black bread,
linens, and wood carvings.

A woman sits at an empty table
apart from the rest.
She wears glasses and a faded print dress.
Gray steaks her once dark hair.
A sign advertises tarot readings for 20 litas[1].
Few bother with this crazy old Latvian woman,
when there are restaurants to open and hotels to build.

Townsfolk whisper rumors of a love affair with a soldier,
an unwanted pregnancy,
a scandal, and a fresh start in a new town.
Others insinuate a little girl divulged
a forest brothers'[2] camp,
and the KGB relocated her for her own protection.

If you stop at her table,
you will notice tremors in her hands.
Doctors say they're due to tick-borne encephalitis
contracted in a Latvian forest
and the lack of prompt antibiotic treatment,
but Anna will tell you it's the gift of the trees
that allows her to see the future.

She says the trees give mankind their bodies for lumber.
They wept at being used to build Jesus' cross.
These tears became amber for jewelry.
She warns we must always be grateful for the forest's gifts
and not abuse its generosity.

Don't let her upset you.
She's only a crazy woman,
a bit of local color for the tourists.
Stop at one of the new cafés on the edge of town.
Have some *cepelinai* or *blynas*.[3]
A few of the fine local beers will help you forget.

1. About $5.
2. Rebels who lived in the forest after the Soviet takeover.
3. Zeppelin shaped dumplings or crepes.

The Dogs of Argentina

follow us all day
after only a pat on the head.
Not the pampered purebreds
walked in packs of twelve through
wealthy Buenos Aires neighborhoods,
but the strays who beg at cafes
like desperate mothers shouldering
hungry infants to diners' tables.

Eduardo, the German Shepherd, sticks by our heels
through the streets and parks of Villa Gesell
and growls when scratching his back against bushes.
What do I owe him for such loyalty? A plane ticket
to America? Space on my living room floor?
He rests a warm, comforting paw on my leg
when Lauren goes to buy him a snack
and receives the empanadas with grace
and a dainty reach of the tongue.

What of the dogs who do not accept poverty with humility?
Zulu jumps leaving paw prints on our shirts
and tears across the street to steal plastic bottles
from the trash for rough-and-tumble games of tug of war,
sharp teeth millimeters from naked fingers.
Charismatic with a gray Che Guevara beard on his muzzle
Zulu inspires other strays to gather like demonstrators
waving red, hammer-and-sickle banners.
Landowner dogs bark wild with rage behind fences.

Announced by a chorus of howls Lauren and I arrive
at the Zen center on Calle Ocho. Pine incense,
the sound of bells, a mallet striking a wooden block.
In the serenity of the meditation hall
knees grind into the concrete floor.
The stillness marred by a scratch, whine,
and snuffle under the door.

Mothers of the Disappeared Bookstore, Buenos Aires

The snapshots are unremarkable
save for clothing thirty years out of date.
Some black and white, others color.
These are the victims of the dirty war. The generals,
now ghostly TV images, their faces gray as intestines,
ordered deaths by the thousands. Ordinary people
hustled into Ford Falcons, tortured. Their bodies
tossed from DC-3s into the Atlantic.

But it's not that simple. Photos of Lenin, Castro,
and Che Guevara hang on the bookstore's walls.
I buy a Mothers-of-the-Disappeared T-shirt for my mom
and pray it doesn't' become a prophecy in Bush's America.
Outside pounding drums. Marchers with red flags.
Do ghosts of Ford Falcons still cruise these streets?

We wait on the sidewalk, while tens of thousands pass.
"*Muchas gentes*," a shop owner says. I nod.
The drums – boom, ba boom, ba boom. Girls
selling socialist newspapers. Marchers
with banners wide as the Avenida de Mayo.
Lauren takes out her camera. The flash!
Rows of men with clubs bring up the rear,
their faces disguised with bandanas or keffiyehs.

We cross to Café Tortoni. Fine china. Cloth napkins.
Waiters in tuxedos. Photos of celebrities on mahogany walls.
I drop a submarine-shaped chocolate in my cup of hot milk.
Lauren sips coffee and says, "This is the best night of my
life."

Borges' House

Buenos Aires
                    wooden door
                         brass plaque
                             a request
                                   Do not to bother the tenants

I recite
     14 words   40 syllables
a magic spell written with a jaguar's pen
     14 words   40 syllables
& I'm inside

Mirrors   shadows
a map of a fictional country

Under white sheets
                         simulacra
a knife fighter
             carnation behind his ear
sorcerer with a bull's head
the man whose father was a dream

Two Borges argue
              the nature of the soul

In the library
         cach book
                 a random permutation
                       of all letters that fit its pages

At least one
              contains this poem

Neruda's House

Model ships, ships in bottles, a boat he never sailed,
mounted fish, concrete seahorse, toy wooden whale,
black-and-white film of him
with newsboy cap and bulbous nose
examining some rusty gear or carved figure from Bali,
portholes, astrolabes, brass ship's compass,
the seashell collection he resumed after giving the first away,
Neruda once saw a plank drifting in the ocean.
"Here comes my desk," he said.

What's left of that Communist
who once fled over the mountains on horseback?
Beetles and butterflies, green ink stains,
wooden masks, narwhal tusk, Pinochet's iron fist,
the colored drinking glasses that made water taste better.
I can almost see him leaning elbows on the zinc bar
Campari in hand.

Stirrups, penguin, steam locomotive –
all iron and eccentric wheels,
ceramic cow, Lorca's ghost, 2000 Spanish refugees,
pink Coro-Coro bird embalmed wings spread,
paintings of watermelons, Whitman, Matilde
with Karl Marx hidden in her hair, some tourist saying,
"Neruda, he was just a poet. Right?"

Just a poet, just a singer of the commonplace:
tuna, tomatoes, Valparaiso's ramshackle tin roofs.
Just a voice for laborers and the poor:
fishermen, peddlers, the bum stealing beer
from an outdoor café. They now sleep
under the roof of his words
and dream like he did
of a fifth-floor heliport
gateway to the stars.

Santiago's Notorious Beer Thief

Elite detectives
  examine empty mugs for clues
while the city lives in fear
its mayor pleading
  for reinforcements

Citizens cower
  behind locked doors
Those who brave the night
  find llamas in bulletproof vests
  stray dogs with police radios
  roadblocks, ID checks
  armed guards at restaurants

Who is he?
When will he strike again?

At the outdoor café
  you only looked away for an instant
Then automatic weapons fire, smell of cordite
Bearded man in dirty clothes
  wiping his lips
  running
  dodging a fusillade of bullets

You stare open mouthed
your glass

  empty

Bird Watching

Bells chime the noon melody from St. Mary's Cathedral,
a European pattern of granite stamped
in Sydney's landscape. Magpies, their white markings
resembling clay painted
on Aboriginal bodies, whistle and howl,
"We've been here since the Dreamtime,"
from gum trees' sinuous branches.

I see few wild marsupials.
Instead, winged creatures act as envoys
for this place's gods.
Inch-long bogong moths greet me at my hotel,
while birds ferry my credentials to Baiame[1],
birds with faces painted like Chinese opera characters,
red and blue parrots, cockatoos, pink and gray galahs,
and sacred ibises[2] walking on stilts
probing grass with curved beaks.
Beside a path lined with photos
the size of Captain Cook's sails
I wait for a feather authorizing safe passage
to drift from the clouds.

1. Aboriginal Great Father Spirit
2. A misnomer. The bird in Sydney is an Australian white
ibis. The sacred ibis refers to an African species.

After Basho

Even in Australia
the kookaburra's cry
makes me long for Australia.

Ode to a Wombat

Friendly-faced ambassador
little
   smiling
    bear
button eyes   tennis-ball nose

Clumsy civil engineer
too distracted
by choco Tim Tam dreams
to shore up collapsing burrows
Always emerging from cave-ins
disheveled   dusty   puzzled

Unconcerned
that cousin Koala won the popular vote
Wombat takes life as it comes
munching grass   rolling in dust
turning on her back   stubby legs bent
to nap in the early morning sun

Perceval

My feet, sore from weeks of walking concrete, carried me past Federation Square with its buildings like silver blocks of cheese melted in the sun. I'd stopped earlier at the Über Tickets office and learned that "Acrobat" and "Jimmy" were sold out. I looked at my watch and picked up the pace. Haste stoked my body's furnace. The parka I'd bought at the Queen Victoria Market trapped my sweat, making the air near my chest humid as a rainforest. Something tore in my left foot. I stopped and sat on some stone steps. Distances in Melbourne seemed much shorter on the map.

To the northwest the setting sun touched the horizon. A beam of its orange light shined through the scattered clouds and illuminated a doorway surrounded by red and yellow banners announcing "Half Price Tickets." I looked at my watch again. I could spare a few minutes to take a look.

Inside birds' howls and whistles replaced the traffic sounds from Swanston Street. I smelled eucalyptus. The woman behind the counter wore a gray blouse that opened to reveal a glimpse of her flat chest. Sleeves trailed from her wrists like wisps of vapor. Despite her wooly gray curls, her radiant skin appeared smooth and youthful.

"How you going?" she asked between chomps on her gum.

"Good. Have any tickets for tomorrow's Melbourne Arts Festival?"

"Sorry. Day of the show only."

She fingered her curled long black nails.

Someone coughed, drawing my attention to the back room behind the counter. Through the opening I saw the bandaged leg of a man lying atop a litter.

I turned back to the clerk. "That's okay. I'm going to a poetry reading tonight. I'll come back tomorrow."

"No worries."

I walked a few blocks, thought better of it, and doubled back to check the cross street, but the banners had vanished. It took an hour to limp to North Fitzroy and find the address I sought. It turned out to be an empty storefront, nothing but broken concrete and two-by-fours behind a dirty plate-glass window.

The next day I searched up and down Swanston for the ticket office but found nothing worth noting except an Aboriginal pissing on the wall of St. Paul's Cathedral. I walked to the RMIT bookstore.

"Know where the half-price ticket office is?"

"It's on the Bourke Street Mall. Isn't it?"

I walked six blocks south to the mall without finding the office. I asked again at a tourist information booth.

"Half price tickets." The old man in a bowtie cleared his throat. "On Swanston, near the Town Hall." He drew the route on a map.

I followed the green felt tip line and found nothing but a concrete wall.

"Excuse me, sir." A man with a grizzled beard and tattered clothes approached. "Want to buy *The Big Issue*? It's only three dollars."

I handed him some coins. "You know of a half price ticket office near here?"

"Old business partner of mine used to run one a few years back." He scratched his chin. "That was before he got in a knife fight with an Aboriginal. Tip broke off in his leg. Doctors said it was too close to the femoral artery to operate. Left him lame and too weak to run the business, so he had to close it down."

"That's funny," I said. "I was just there last night, and there was a sick guy on a cot in the back room."

"Did you ask him how he was going?"

"Naw, I didn't want to bother him."

"Pity." The vendor handed me the magazine.

I sensed that I'd stumbled into a cosmic mystery. The answer could free humanity from the tyranny of excessive service charges and handling fees. But I didn't have time to chase phantoms. I had to be back at work Monday morning to finish some Gantt charts before my deadline. I set off toward Über Tickets on Little Bourke Street, and certainty.

Rainforest Samadhi[1]

Eungella National Park, Queensland, Australia

Even in this magical place
two thugs named Anger and Worry
break beer bottles   dump garbage
laugh at my misfortune

There is a path they cannot follow
the path of no thought
palm trees   sword ferns
scattering of pink leaves
simply being at one with the forest
that doesn't care about my petty concerns

But
the forest is all petty concerns.
A few seeds   scrap of meat   a stolen $90
no difference.
Terrified of confrontation
Platypus fumes in his den
while Brush Turkey runs off with the spoils.
Cockatoo
screams from the treetop
"Thief! Come back here!"

Quietude is not enough.
Conflict, not enough.
Something more

1. Samadhi is another term for meditation.

Treaty House at Waitangi[1]

Across a perfect lawn a skeleton of stained wood
supports the white A-frame.
A carving of Kupe, the discoverer,
grins with paddle in hand from the gable over the doorway.
He gazes at a white flagpole, standing like a ship's mast,
on the promontory overlooking islands that float
like greenstone canoes on the sapphire bay.

I slip off my shoes. Inside socks glide
over the smooth wooden floor. Fierce faces
of Maori ancestors threaten with protruding tongues,
glare with mother-of-pearl eyes from carved beams.
So this is where the British and Maori signed the treaty!

Only it's not. In my rush to the 1940 Maori meeting hall
I passed the Treaty House without a second glance.
Humble like compromise, the boxy white structure
looks like an office, not the birthplace of a nation.

Humble too was the house's owner, James Busby.
Lacking George Armstrong Custer's halo of golden hair
and thunder of Spencer repeating rifles,
Busby negotiated with the Maori chiefs.

No Trail of Tears, no Wounded Knee --
No thunderous brass band for Busby
only courtrooms and bankruptcy
Nations do not honor heroes with no blood on their hands.

1. With an enlightened attitude for its time the 1840 Treaty
of Waitangi guaranteed the indigenous Maori's property and
rights while allowing the British to govern New Zealand. James
Busby was responsible for drafting much of the treaty.

Looking for Hinemoa[1]

I return to New Zealand, this time alone.
In Te Anau a little girl
hands me the key to a motel room with sliding glass door
switches on wall sockets, two spigots on the sink,
water boiler and milk for Earl Grey tea,
Sky Cable, Maori TV, McLeod's Daughters, Sea Patrol,
the lake and steamboat framed in my window

Round speed-limit signs, one-lane bridges, driving mountain
roads on the left, windshield wipers when I reach for turn
signals, Cherry blossoms, Southern Alps rock and ice,
fern trees, red tussock, granite scoured by glaciers,
the chill turquoise water of the Tasman Sea, black swans,
pukeko birds, quail, red-billed seagulls, ducks
with sergeant's stripes, tree avalanches, waterfalls, the tui
that knocked himself silly flying into my picture window,
dirty blue ice melting into gray runoff from the Franz Josef
Glacier, Lambs gambol while sheep fatten for the slaughter.

Bumper bars, purple carrots, Hindi music videos, meat pies
kept hot in glass cases, feijoa juice, long blacks, flat whites,
the fern drawn in cappuccino's foam, New World, Four
Square, Whitcoulls Books The Plunket Society, Helen Clark's
red lipstick, How you going? kumara, give way, tramping,
zipper tape, An entrée is an appetizer and a main is an en-
trée. Cheers!

Adventure sports, outrageous fashions, a college turned
into an art center the *moko* on a woman's chin, a paddle
boat shaped like a tricycle, on the street a guy in a bathrobe
and shower cap promoting cereal, the two-way car, a slide
shaped like a dinosaur, two tired Dutch kayakers, the young
Spanish woman rolling cigarettes on the beach
I feel so old. No one will ever want me.

1. According to Maori legend Hinemoa swam naked across Lake
Rotorua to be with her lover.

Yang Guifei Sings the Blues

Hong Kong 1998 - A year and a half after its return to China

Not much has changed
apart from a few red flags with five stars.
Yang Guifei[1] wears jeans and running shoes
and sings old songs of forbidden love
under naked light bulbs at night on Temple Street.
A red and blue striped plastic tarp
shelters the six-man orchestra seated on the asphalt.

General Guan Di takes the stage
holding a bamboo staff.
If you enjoy his song,
slip a few bucks into the straw basket.
Yang Guifei will smile
and offer you a stool to sit on.

Live chickens wait for the butcher's cleaver
in cages beneath red neon lights.
Decapitated fish wriggle in plastic tubs
and stain the water with their blood.
Hui Neng[2] stands in gassho[3] at the entrance to the market
with his shaved head and brown robe
to witness this killing demanded by a hungry city.
Drop a coin into his alms bowl.
He'll show you his California driver's license
and give you an amulet for your protection.
Monkey[4] imagines searching the streets
for a fruit stand selling peaches.
He wanders past Chinese herb shops,
outdoor restaurants,
video displays in camera store windows,
the green and white Star Ferry terminal, and
      lights
            lights
                    lights
                          mirrored off the bay.

Li Po[5] seems ready to fall off the pier
reaching for this reflection of Hong Kong.
Monkey distracts him with a few dollars,
paid for an autographed book of poetry
and a tale of ancient Chinese heroes.

1. Yang Guifei and General Guan Di are figures from legend
   that appear in Chinese opera.
2. Hui Neng is a famous Buddhist monk.
3. Hands with palms together as if praying.
4. Monkey is an imaginary character, who got into a great
   deal of trouble with the Jade Emperor for eating the
   peaches of immortality.
5. Li Po was a Chinese poet. According to legend he died
   when stepping of his boat to reach for the reflection of the
   moon on the water.

Thunder God

Sometimes gods masquerade in human form. I met one of them, Lei Shen, in Guangdong province.

Our tour group visits one of the few parks in China where fireworks are allowed. Chan, our guide, is at the age when a young man thinks blowing stuff up is about the coolest thing there is to do (well, maybe the second coolest). He offers to buy fireworks, if we come up with 200 yuan (roughly $25). Chinese, American, English, Australian; guys just love to blow stuff up. The women don't complain too much either. We collect the money, and Chan walks over to the fireworks stand to bargain.

While Chan arranges the evening's entertainment, I try to make time with the English nurse Peggy, hoping to score a bit more entertainment than everyone else. She wears jeans and a loose turquoise blouse. Mild acne colors her face with a faint pink blush. Curly blonde hair falls just short of her shoulders.

She says, "I'm staying at a heroin addiction treatment center in Hong Kong. My friend works there."

"Don't you worry about the patients stealing your things?"

"It's pretty safe. By the way, do you know where the internment camp for the Vietnamese boat people is? I think it's somewhere in the New Territories. I want to see it, before I leave."

I don't know where the camp is. I only know I'll get caught and probably deported, if I get within twenty miles of the place. I'm one of those people, who can't get away with anything. She'll be OK, though.

One of the beggars approaches and mutters something like, "Eh, eh." He shows us a cigarette lighter and makes a motion with his hands like smoking. I shrug my shoulders and shout, "Sorry, don't have any." I know the extra volume won't make my English easier for him to understand, but that doesn't stop me.

Chan returns with the fireworks and we begin setting them off. Eventually we form a line and fire fusillades of flares from our Roman candles over the lake. The natives watch impassively. It feels rather colonial.

In a gesture of equality and good will I motion to the beggar to light the last firecracker. He does so, and we begin walking back to our hotel. Chan asks me, "Why the beggar?" I can't explain and never get the chance anyway. I hear a loud thunderclap, and rain starts pouring down. Peggy and I run laughing to our hotel, pass the dumbfounded doormen, and leave the rest of the tourists behind huddled under umbrellas.

Cruising the Lijiang

An armada of tour boats plies the Li River.
Yesterday's badgering by a plague of peddlers
left me too annoyed to enjoy today's cruise.
Each huckster boasted of the river's pure water
and hawked paintings of its rock formations:
Elephant Hill, Camel Hill, Bat Hill...

I view the scenery from the railing
and chat with an Italian.
"There sure are lots of Italians in China. Why?"
"Why not?"

I feel a vibration. The boat's run aground.
A voice from the loudspeaker orders us to disembark.
We cross the gangway onto the rocky bank.
I distance myself from the boat, when I see deck hands
smoking cigarettes while trying to stop
diesel fuel gushing from the punctured hull
into the formerly pure water of the Li river.

Best Meal in China

*Xian - ancient Chinese capital. Arab traders, who traveled
the Silk Road, settled here. The flat countryside resembles
Kansas except for the emperors buried under earthen
mounds, terra cotta warriors, and stone wall surrounding
the city. A green sign with white Chinese and Arabic script
announces the entrance to the Moslem quarter.*

Hungry, I roam crowded streets
eyeing vendors cooking in blackened
woks over orange coal fires.
Don't want a diarrhea tour squatting over tile-lined ditches,
so I tango the third world eating dance.
Avoid salad and shellfish. Make sure everything's hot.
Language barrier? Hell, I can't even read the writing!
Tempted to return to my hotel in despair.
Oh, that café looks all right.
I order in clumsy Mandarin
and enter the green and white cement dining room.
Cups of wooden chopsticks blossom
like flowers from each table.

A four-year-old girl with Asian features
and reddish-brown hair smiles at me from nearby.
America enters wearing a "Just do it" T-shirt,
sits next to me, and orders a Pepsi, "no ice."
He wants to know if the girl's name is Freedom.
I ask, but she just hides her face.
Her father brings a generous plate of noodles
spiced with the words of Mohammed and Confucius.
Costs 50 cents. Best deal in China!

Bowing at Chogye-sa

Seoul - Lunar New Year's Day

Hundreds crowd the Main Hall
to face the multitude of Buddhas
painted on the Wall of Heroes.
Strings of beads entwine fingers.
Brown cotton mats
insulate shoeless feet from cold linoleum
and cushion bowing bodies.
Worshippers kneel,
touch foreheads to floor,
and rise;
only to lay themselves flat
again and again.
I sit in the corner
my back straight with reluctance.
Would I, a foreigner, create a spectacle?

In my hotel room the next morning
I realize the truth is all around,
only I choose not to see.
I've known this all along.
I make three prostrations on the plush gold carpet,
using my body to place truth before selfish desires.
Oops, wrong direction!
I meant to face the temple.
Three bows north. Might as well
tick off the other points of the compass.

The words of a tour guide come back to me.
"We believe in five directions, not just four."
I pause
then bow to the center.

Obon

Japanese offer to help the dead,
who return for a week in August.
A half dozen people cluster around a Buddhist monk
by the Arashiyama train station at dusk.
Heads turn
when I walk past on my way to the celebration.

The neighborhood dons its finest kimono
for tonight's gathering by the river.
Bonfires hang from fishing boats
to attract fish for tethered cormorants to catch.

A river front restaurant serves the local delicacy, *yudofu*[1]
I sit by a group of businessmen.
Sake reddens faces. I hear Alcohol's raised voice.
The waitress appreciates my need for stillness
and moves me closer to the window.

Far from the boasting of the salary men
silence summons memories from before time began.
Orange flames reflect
the birth and death of stars from the water.
I glimpse light through the narrow gap
between the door to the absolute and its frame,

but it's not time to step through.
I walk back to the station,
wave goodbye to the monk and his entourage,
and savor the last moments of this warm quiet night.
A drunk joins me on the deserted platform.
He mutters a song, finds a broom, and sweeps.
I hear crossing bells
and the distant sound of the approaching train.

1. Simmered tofu

Hiroshima Forty Years After

I don't know what to expect as I follow the Enola Gay's path along the river. After departing the train in Hiroshima days before the nuclear-physics conference, August heat sticks the shirt to my sweaty back. Guzzling bottled green tea and following a tourist map, I navigate to the site of the bombing, passing shops, restaurants, and modern buildings along the way. Well-wishers have built statues and memorials, but I sense a hurt beneath the goodwill. Eventually, I arrive at the Hiroshima Carp baseball stadium across from the famous dome. Ground zero.

Circling the dome's skeletal steel frame, I snap pictures - click, wind, click. The Peace Bell's somber chime warns of some grim future but children laugh and play while standing in line to swing the striking log at its bronze body. By the mountains of paper cranes, left behind by the crowds at last week's anniversary, a man asks for a donation. I give him twenty bucks and sign his list of donors. He wants to know what a physicist does.

The main museum displays stopped watches, melted statues, and other curiosities. I enter a side building to view survivors' drawings. Most were not artists so many pictures look as if grade school children made them. However, children do not draw corpses by the river, babies at the breasts of dead mothers, or victims whose clothes and even skin were burned off by the nuclear flash. The nine hundred paper cranes, a girl with radiation-induced leukemia folded before dying, fill a jar. According to folklore, she would have earned a cure, if she'd made it to a thousand so visitors fold cranes in her honor. A screen depicts the Bodhisattva of Compassion on one panel and a mushroom cloud on the other, implying that compassion exists even in the midst of destruction if only we can see.

I linger wondering if I can do something, offer some assistance. Nothing comes to mind. The admission-free theater at the animation festival shows commercials for Toyota, Honda, and Sony as if buying Japanese products could atone. My presence is futile. Fleeing this city, I escape to the station where crossing bells wail like air-raid sirens. I board the train and return to the emotional safety of Osaka, where I will clamp my mouth shut when a bearded, Los Alamos scientist raises his voice to expound that America must have the will to use nuclear weapons again to a group of shocked Japanese.

Most attendees don't go to Hiroshima. The few who do never see the survivors' paintings. Still, it's not that simple. At Himeji, between Hiroshima and Osaka, I saw the White Crane Castle's secret rooms. If defeated, the defenders were to hide inside and then burst out in a suicidal attack to slaughter as many victors as possible. That mindset that gave us Pearl Harbor and the Rape of Nanking. So yes, I would have done anything to end the war once and for all, if I had been Harry Truman. I just wish the world could be different somehow.

The Enola Gay lies in pieces in a Washington museum,
while beside a shattered dome
someone contemplates knowledge's misuse
and mourns the victims of humanity's folly.

Much later I wonder,
whether we can only find peace
within our hearts.
Can you hear the end of war?

Nara Park[1]

Beside the Kasuga Shrine there's a wedding.
The bride dresses in white,
so she can be dyed any color her husband wishes.
My view is blocked by a sea of in-laws.
I feel like an intruder holding my camera
waiting for an opening
and anxious to capture this scene of traditional Japan.
The wedding photographer positions the couple.
He places the groom's left and right foot precisely,
and turns his head to the proper angle.
His assistant stuffs Kleenex under the groom's jacket
and creases his *hakama*[2].
Meanwhile, Botchan[3] and his friend drag their feet
through patterns in the carefully raked gravel.
A woman opens a door to the shrine
and exits.
I notice a sign
advertising fortunes in English for only 200 yen.
At last there's a clearing.
Snap.
I've got my picture.
I can go now.

1 Nara was the Japanese capital around 800 A. D. There are
  lots of Buddhist temples and Shinto shrines there.
2 A hakama is a pair of traditional skirt like pants worn by
  Japanese men.
3 Botchan is a nickname for a Japanese boy

Haiku & Tanka

Gingko leaves falling.
One spirals like a glider.
This must be Japan.

Melancholy day.
Gray skies at Warei Jinja.
Leaves fall one by one.

A small donation
given at a Shinto shrine.
I walk on a bit
and meet a little school girl
whose English phrase is, "Thank you."

Zentsuji Temple

Zentsuji is the pilgrimage site on Shikoku Island close to where the monk Kobo Daishi was born in 774 AD. I take the *Kaidan-Meguri* walk under a building called the *Mieido*. I enter the pitch-black tunnel and place my left hand on the wall. Blindly I stumble forward with only the contact of my hand to guide me. The passage twists and turns. I know nothing more than where to place my next step. It's like searching for the temple in the first place; like life itself. Eventually I reach a chamber. A pressure switch trips the lights and recorded chanting. A statue of Kobo Daishi looks at me with a benevolent expression. I rest and admire the paintings on the walls. Then it's time to return to the darkness and take the next step into the unknown.

The temple bell sounds.
A swinging striking log
the pilgrim's only trace.

Backstage at the Noh Play

A shrill flute, drumbeat – boom!
Something primal, duty's austere voice
rises from deep in the belly –
a belly that prefers a knife to dishonor.
With bent knees and straight back a lone dancer
pivots and stomps. Muscles tremble to hold tradition.
In the background a castle donjon rises like a pelican
of plaster and wood from sloping stonewalls.
Feudalism's ghost nods appreciation from the window.

Mrs. Inoue's high school girls have already
finished their chorus and carried off book bags
of teddy bears and Tom Cruise dreams.
Behind the curtain Noh players clip cell phones
to their belts instead of swords.
The only duels they see are on TV.
Women in costumes from *The Tale of Genji*
discuss J-Pop and U2's latest tour.

Turn anywhere in Japan and find a contradiction –
old people nodding to a jazz fusion band at a Shinto shrine,
a woman removing thigh-length platform boots to step
onto grass mats. "What a Friend We have in Jesus" drifts
through the walls of a museum housing Buddhist statues.
Uniformed teenagers gather at a baseball diamond
three blocks from rice wine offerings and chants to the gods.
"Hey batter! Hey batter! Hey batter! Swing!"

I turn for a final picture before hiking
to a garden with a 400-year-old tea house.
Which is the real Japan?
Could a stage exist without bamboo supports?
Would the players gather without the stage?
Holding his fan like a sword the dancer turns.
The shutter clicks. I leave the castle grounds
and enter the twenty-first century.

Time

The flight from Osaka to Los Angeles will arrive before it
        leaves.
I read a book that says allowing the future to affect the past
resolves all the paradoxes of quantum mechanics.
The student next to me talks about the kaon[1] experiment
he will be analyzing at Fermilab.
As we cross the international dateline,
I half expect to land in Vancouver twelve years ago
and think of all, I would have done differently
given a second chance.

1 Kaon decay is the only known subatomic process that vio-
lates time reversal symmetry.

Last Day

As each vacation's end approaches,
I'm once again a boy on Sunday night
just hours from my dreaded return to junior high.
I make the best of the time left.

Serendipity! The Portland Corgi Walk
hundreds of stubby-legged dogs, eyes shining,
ears tall as microwave towers

A sunny afternoon on Brussels' Grand Place
cobblestones, guild halls,
Neo Gothic house of Hapsburg kings.
European TV all night
Weather reports from Turkey. Turkey!
Belgian ale and Arab pastries for breakfast
– pistachio, honey, rose water

Dublin throws me a going-away party
with a musical in my hotel – man and woman
singing about the death of their love.
Yeat's ghost leads me around the corner
to his Abbey Theatre. A cabby
shows me his hurling stick at the airport.

Feeling like an old Asia hand after five weeks,
I climb the ramp to a 747. The boy in front asks,
"How many years you been here?
I've been for three."

Hong Kong, a typhoon buys me an extra day.
"Would you like some green tea, sir?"
the valet turns down my bedspread.
"Why yes! Yes, I would!"

Loose Ends

So much I didn't tell you:
women shedding clothes on my birthday, plunging
into the Pacific waves glowing from luminous algae,
how the mangosteen is the best fruit
except maybe for Japan's white peach
or Pacific Northwest thimble berries, tart red.

Shouts of
"Shoe shine! Shoe shine!" in O'Hare airport,
an old guy pirouetting on roller blades
in a 7-Eleven parking lot,
the Northwest Indian legend of a man
turned into Siwash Rock as a reward for generosity.

The Three Sisters in Australia's Blue Mountains
also turned to stone, this time by their shaman father
who died in battle before reversing the spell.
Cicadas big as humming birds, the sun rising on the right,
a sandal big as a couch, radio station 3RRR,
taking curves along the Great Ocean Road,
Millie the wombat clawing a furrow in the dirt
while I crooned and scratched her rump.

Platanos rellenos - bananas stuffed with chicken,
Lithuanian dumplings shaped like zeppelins,
twenty kinds of empanadas in Argentina,
In Spain a tortilla is a potato omelet
and *horchata* is made with almonds.
Squid on a stick, *kaiseki* - sushi in tiny chest of drawers,
a box of soy milk *hot* in Macao,
the pizza I cooked for Kyoko in a fish broiler
and Koji worrying I'd overcook the ham,
six small cups of strong oolong tea in Hong Kong
and the roar of the crowd at dim sum,
a waitress raising her voice so I'd understand Mandarin.

Farmer Yang who got a paltry $30
for discovering the Terra Cotta Warriors,
the guide in a Hard Rock Café Beijing T-Shirt
listening to the Cranberries when we drove to Ningbo,
an English teacher in a Mao jacket
who lived in Louisiana but never saw New Orleans,
Confucian scholars in Seoul waving,
the Red Army veteran who played me taped Estonian protest
songs, Santiago's notorious beer thief, stray dogs &
men walking a dozen dogs each in Buenos Aires,
Gardelito tangoing with Lauren in the park,
a Mayan hammock peddler
who taught me to say no in Yucatec,
dreadlocked teens doing Capoeira summersaults in Geneva,
the shy smile of a hotel owner
herding a bunny into her room,
a monk with a gold tooth carrying an arrow in Kyoto,
the woman who ran off to a Japanese train station
and returned ten minutes later with a map to my hotel,
Kyoko's 80-year-old father bowing
on my leaving his house of tatami and Amida Buddha.
"Please take care of yourself."

Bullfights in an ancient coliseum in southern France,
a Burger King by a Roman gate in Germany,
bears in Berne, the fox in Jackie's garden,
incomprehensible British phrases like "traffic calming",
midsummer night - a rowboat with a torch
welcoming the sun after its brief dip under the Baltic,
parks named for poets, poets on money – a Lydia dollar,
Language is the nation. The love of their newfound freedom,
a bar and a sauna too, sauna – physician of the poor,
slot cars left there by a touring rock star,
the owner's dog who went with him to scout film locations
(Helsinki – Moscow's stunt double).

Hong Kong – the smell of kerosene,
the longest escalator in the world,
red and blue plastic tarps everywhere,
strolling on balmy November evenings,
Hanoi Street, neon lights, dinner at an outdoor café.

Rolling down a hill in an inflated ball in Rotorua,
and me chief of the bus for a Maori ceremony,
Mt. Ruapeha white goddess
admiring her reflection in Lake Taupo,
"It's beautiful here," says Lauren. "Let's stay."

A Foreigner at Home

My friends spend $100 on tolls and parking
to drive me to the immaculate Japanese airport.
Clerks bow and welcome me, when I enter gift shops.
Passengers wait quietly
then form efficient lines to board our plane.

I arrive at LAX after a ten-hour flight.
The customs inspector says "No problem,"
when I declare my tea and pickled plums.
My connecting flight is delayed.
I can't get the clerk's attention for a slice of pizza.
She's too busy talking on the phone.
I sit in the waiting area by the gate
and look out the window at the brown LA sky.
"Aren't you glad to be back?
America's the greatest country on earth."
Someone always says this,
whenever I return from overseas.

I take Japanese coins from my pockets and examine them.
The years date from the emperor's coronation.
American coins say "Liberty."
I'm thankful
not to measure my life by the pulse of kings or tyrants.

Dressed in a pilot's uniform,
America sits on a bar stool knocking back
vengeance and self-righteousness on the rocks.
He gets up,
        staggers to the cockpit,
                and sits at the controls
                        of the plane that will take me home.

The flight attendant calls my row. I walk through the gate.
Once on board, I search for an overhead bin
large enough to hold my fears for America's future.

Jon Wesick is a regional editor of the *San Diego Poetry Annual*. He's published hundreds of poems and stories in journals such as the *Atlanta Review, Berkeley Fiction Review, Metal Scratches, Pearl, Slipstream, Space and Time, Tales of the Talisman*, and *Zahir*. The editors of *Knot Magazine* nominated his story *"The Visitor"* for a Pushcart Prize. His poem "Meditation Instruction" won the Editor's Choice Award in the 2016 Spirit First Contest. Another poem "Bread and Circuses" won second place in the 2007 African American Writers and Artists Contest. "Richard Feynman's Commute" shared third place in the 2017 Rhysling Award's short poem category. Jon is the author of the poetry collection *Words of Power, Dances of Freedom* as well as several novels and most recently the short-story collection *The Alchemist's Grandson Changes His Name*. http://jonwesick.com

A master of vivid detail, Jon Wesick "dissolves the membrane of time and space." In California, we are escorted by dolphins "like old surfers reborn / with complimentary wetsuits" and meet Elvis impersonators ("No one will pay them to be themselves."). We travel on to Buddhist wisdom, particle physics, Yucatan, ancestral Estonia, Buenos Aires with the ghosts of the Disappeared, China, Japan, and Australia. Beauty and suffering do not annihilate like matter and antimatter, but combine in endless permutations. Throughout, "America," in the guise of this or that actual person, appears in brief, disquieting cameos. The landscape is both sensory and psychological, a proverbial feast of memory where the horrors of history are also served.

~ Oriana Ivy, author of prize-winning *April Snow, From the New World, How to Jump from a Moving Train*.

If you love poems of place, you will find Paradise when you read Jon Wesick's new book A Foreigner, Wherever I Go. The poems in this book combine lush details and vivid characters with the unrelenting yet compassionate eye of the speaker as he travels from the west to the east coasts of the United States and back again and then to the Netherlands and England and Ireland and France and on to Argentina and Australia and Hong Kong, mainland China, and Japan. In these pages you'll find Anne Frank, Neruda, Oscar Wilde, and Basho; you'll visit Hiroshima, the Li River, Sydney, The Mothers of the Disappeared Bookstore, Estonia, Lithuania— the list goes on. Wesick's poetry is muscular in its descriptive abilities and lyric in its reflective awareness of unity with yet separation from all he encounters. This book is well worth reading.

Steve McDonald, author of *Credo* and *House of Mirrors*

A Foreigner, Wherever I Go takes the reader across & around the globe with humor & a sincere devotion to exploring the character & personalities of the cultures encountered. Many of these poems, written by a young man traveling extensively for the first time, have an air of naiveté that offers a refreshing vison at a time when the world's dissimilar cultures, although seeming accessible, regain much of their unique mystery in these intimate quotidian rendezvouse

Roger Aplon -Editor: *Waymark-Voices of the Valley*
Latest poetry collection: *Mustering What's Left – Selected & New Poems 1976-2017*
Soon from Unsolicited Press: *The Omnipotent Sorcerer*

Are you ready for a wild ambling trip around the world without an airplane ticket? Well, cruise through these pages and you will meet the world! There is no beginning or middle or end...it flies effortlessly through the lives of the people who interacted with the everchanging bubble of trans world flights. Fasten your seat belts.....See you soon!

Chris Vannoy Beat Poet Laureate of the United States 2019.